W9-CBH-064

just **kids**

Pictures, Poems and Other Silly
Animal Stuff Just for Kids

Includes
fascinating facts
about young animals
for parents to read
to their
young animals!

WILLOW CREEK PRESS

compiled by Bonnie Louise Kuchler

© Erwin and Peggy Bauer

For Jill and Nate,
who make life fun.

Acknowledgements:
Thanks to my daughter, Jill,
for unending inspiration;
thanks to my son, Nate,
for sharing my love of wildlife.
Thanks, Kiddos, for cheering me on.

Published by Willow Creek Press
P.O. Box 147, Minocqua, Wisconsin 54548
www.willowcreekpress.com

Cataloging-in-Publication Data

Just kids : pictures, poems & other silly animal
    stuff just for kids! / compiled by Bonnie Louise
    Kuchler.
        p. cm.
    Summary: A collections of quotations about
    friendship, emotions, and other matters accom-
    panied by photographs of animals.
    ISBN 1-57223-598-5 (hardcover : alk. paper)
    1. Conduct of life--Quotations, maxims, etc.--
    Juvenile literature. 2. Animals--Pictorial works-
    -Juvenile literature. [1. Conduct of life--
    Quotations, maxims, etc. 2. Quotations.
    3. Animals.] I. Kuchler, Bonnie Louise, 1958-
PN6084.C556J87 2003
158.1--dc21

                            2003000111

Printed in Canada

Snowflakes and fingerprints-
You'll always find-
Each one is different,
        one of a kind.

And just like a snowflake
This, too, is true,
No one else is exactly like you!

Harp Seals live in the northern Atlantic and Arctic oceans where it is very cold. Baby harp seals are born with a soft, white fur coat that helps them blend into the snow. They will lose this fur after two or three weeks. It turns dark when they are able to swim along with their mothers.

Whatever you are,
Be a good one.

— Abraham Lincoln

This baby bird is a Black-browed Albatross, a large bird that lives in the sea. These birds nest on islands in the ocean. A chick like this one won't leave the nest until it is almost one year old. Once it leaves the nest, a young bird may not return to its home island until it is at least five years old.

These Wood Duck chicks were born surrounded by trees. Although you may see most ducks on the water or flying over your head, wood ducks make their nests in tree cavities left by woodpeckers or squirrels. The opening to the tree nest must be no bigger than four inches across, and the space inside must be large enough to hold 11 babies!

Be a good listener. Your ears will never get you into trouble.

—Frank Tyger

If you've anything to do
Do it with all your might
Don't let trifles hinder you.
If you're sure you're right,
work away.
Do it with all your might.

— Laura Ingalls Wilder

Cheetah cubs have a puffy mane that makes them look much bigger than they are. These playful babies get into lots of trouble, so looking bigger to a predator comes in handy!

Cheetahs can go from 0 to 60 miles per hour in three seconds! How fast can you run in three seconds?

© Art Wolfe / ArtWolfe.com

Open your heart and you will find . . .
we're all angels deep inside.

—Mark Kimball Moulton

Canada Lynx have thick cushions
of hair on the soles of their large
feet. Can you guess why? It's
because they have to walk through
deep snow, and their hairy feet
work like snowshoes to keep them
from sinking into the snow!

You don't have to be perfect to be worth loving.

— Harold S. Kushner

Orangutans are four-handed. Their hands and "feet" are identical, each with four fingers and one short thumb. This makes it easy to swing from tree to tree, but a real pain to walk! As you might imagine, orangutans almost never set "foot" on the ground.

The front paws of a Raccoon have five fingers. Like humans, a raccoon can use its "hands" to do many things. They have even been known to untie ropes and remove lids from jars!

Try, Try Again

'Tis a lesson you should heed,
Try, try again
If at first you don't succeed,
Try, try again.

— T. H. Palmer

Happiness was made to share.

These two Black Bear cubs were born in a winter den. When black bears are just a few months old, they begin to explore the world outside. Newborn cubs weigh less than a pound! How much did you weigh when you were born?

Hurt no living thing;
ladybird, nor butterfly,
Nor moth with dusty wing,
Nor cricket chirping cheerily,
Nor grasshopper so light of leap,
Nor dancing gnat, nor beetle fat,
Nor harmless worms that creep.

— Christina Rossetti

Eastern Cottontails are small rabbits that live in tall grass where they can hide from predators. The rabbits warn each other of danger by thumping the ground with one of their hind feet.

When angry, count
to ten before you speak;
if very angry, 100.

— Thomas Jefferson

Grey Wolves live in a pack with any-
where from two to twenty members.
The pack is like a family. The wolves
communicate with one another by
howling. A wolf can change its call by
sucking in its cheeks, or by curling and
uncurling its tongue. You try it!

© Art Wolfe / ArtWolfe.com

These birds are called Bee-Eaters because of their diet. Some bee-eaters catch up to 225 bees and similar insects a day! They catch bees, wasps, and hornets in mid-flight, then they return to a perch to swallow them whole after squeezing out their venom.

No matter how many friends you have, there is always room for one more.

This Tengmalm's Owl is nocturnal, which means it gets to stay up all night and sleep all day. An owl can see about a hundred times better than you can in the dark, and it has "stealth feathers," so it can fly noiselessly and sneak up on its prey. This owl makes sounds like "Poop," "Wood-whoohd," "zjuck," "oohwack," "kraihk-kwahk," "seeh" and "zuihd"!

The Owl

A wise old owl sat in an oak
The more he heard the less he spoke
The less he spoke the more he heard
Why aren't we all like that wise
old bird?

A Good Place to Sleep

Little bear sleeps in the woods,
in the woods.
Little gull sleeps on the sea.
Little colt sleeps in a big, big field.
Little squirrel sleeps in a tree.
Small fox sleeps in a den, in a den.
A hive is the place for a bee.
But here I am in my very own bed,
And that's the best place for me.

— Margaret Hillert

When Canada Geese go for a family outing, the kids — or goslings, if you prefer — swim in a straight line between their two parents. If the parents sense danger, they stretch out their long necks as close to the water as they can. The next time you see a floating log, you just might want to look twice!

© Marvin Cattoor / The Image Finders

Have confidence that if you
have done a little thing well,
you can do a bigger thing well, too.

— Joseph Storey

Loggerhead Turtles spend much of their time floating on the surface of the water. That's how they sleep! This baby loggerhead is just hatching out of its egg. Its mom laid the egg on the beach, and now the little turtle must crawl over the sand and through the waves into the ocean, where it will live for the rest of its life.

Whenever I feel like
crying,
I smile hard instead!
I turn my sadness upside
down
and stand it on its head!

— David Saltzman

The Japanese
Macaque (say it
"muh-KACK") is
also called the snow
monkey because it
lives farther north
than any other
monkey. Its long,
shaggy hair protects
it from the cold
temperatures.

I planted birdseed in the ground
And wild weeds sprouted all around.
I know it sounds a bit absurd
But I couldn't grow a single bird.

— Brod Bagert

Snow Leopards are very strong.
Leopards weigh about 100 pounds and
can carry an animal over twice that size
high up into the boughs of a tree!
Leopards spend a lot of time in trees;
they eat, store food, sleep, and keep
watch high up in the branches.

You can't make footprints in the sands of time if you're sitting on your butt. And who wants to make buttprints in the sands of time?

— Bob Moawad

Giant Pandas live only in the remote mountains of China, where it is cool and wet all year. Almost every bite of a giant panda's diet is made up of bamboo. They eat up to 30 pounds of bamboo shoots, leaves, and stems in one day!

My best friend is the one who brings out the best in me.

— Henry Ford

Baby whitetail deer are called fawns. Their coats are spotted so that they blend well with grass and bushes. Their moms are very, very careful to hide them from other animals when they go out to eat. Mom may be gone for several hours, but the fawn will lie quietly, hidden from view, and won't even go to the bathroom until she gets back!

Curled into a cradle, this mother Polar Bear naps and shelters her cub. Dense fur and a thick layer of fat protect polar bears from the icy temperatures of their arctic home.

A mountain goes up
A valley goes down
Where does a hug go?
A hug goes around.

— Laura Krauss Melmed

These Bighorn Sheep lambs live in the Rocky Mountains. They can move easily and quickly on uneven ground because their hooves spread out to help them keep their footing. The rough bottoms and hard outer edges of their hooves don't slip as the animals leap from rock to rock.

Think before you speak, and look before you leap.

— Irish proverb

© Donald M. Jones

These animals are Snowshoe Hares. It's hard to tell the difference between a hare and a rabbit. They are similar, but hares are larger than rabbits, with longer hind legs and ears.

An adult snowshoe hare can jump forward as far as ten feet! How far can you jump?

Whatever you say,
Whatever you do,
Bounces off others
And comes back to you.

Like a human baby who sucks his thumb, a baby elephant sucks its trunk! Young elephants are sometimes kept in a group called kindergarten. One adult will babysit the entire group.

So when you're feeling lonely
   or sad
   or bad
   or blue,
remember where
   laughter's hiding . . .
It's hiding inside
   of YOU!

— David Saltzman

Koalas sleep up to 20 hours a day —
yawn — and they rarely need a drink
of water. They get all the water they
need from their food. In fact, the name
'koala' means 'no drink.'

Want to guess how koalas cool
themselves off when they get hot?
They lick their arms, of course!

There's no such thing as
too many hugs.

— Susan E. Schwartz

$\mathcal{S}$mall is beautiful.

— E.F. Schumacher

This is a Mallard Duckling. When a male mallard duck wants to impress a female duck, he wags his tail, dips his bill into the water, flicking his head to send droplets of water flying, then he lifts his rear end out of the water to show off his colorful feathers . . . and if all this doesn't work, he shakes his head from side to side and jumps out of the water!

The only way to have a friend is to be one.

—Ralph Waldo emerson

Most horses in the world are tame, but some horses are born wild, like these two horses. Wild Horses travel in groups of three to twenty animals, and they spend most of the day grazing. A horse's eyes are placed near the sides of its head. It can see almost in a circle without turning its head!

S+omebody loves you deep and true.

Tigers are the largest of all the wild cats, and the Siberian Tiger is the biggest tiger of all. It usually measures about 9 feet long from its nose to the tip of its tail! These two little Siberian tigers have a lot of growing to do! It may seem like all tigers look the same, but did you now that no two tigers have the same pattern of stripes on their coats?

Although each Woodchuck family has a separate den, their burrows are near each other and form a colony. Each den may be up to 30 feet long!

Woodchucks need the wind to blow away mosquitoes, so you'll rarely see them venture out of their comfy homes on calm days.

Nothing is so strong as gentleness.

© Craig Brandt

Nothing's impossible I have found
for when my chin is on the ground,
I pick myself up,
dust myself off,
start all over again.

— Julie Reece Deaver

The Lion has the
mightiest roar of all wild
cats. It can be heard up
to five miles away and
has enough force to
make the ground seem
like it is shaking!

A friend is someone who knows your senstive spots but will never poke you there.

The American Bison is the heaviest land animal in North America. An adult male, called a bull, can weigh more than a ton, and measures about six feet tall at the shoulder. These two young calves will soon grow to look like their parents, and darker hair will grow in to replace their reddish-brown coats.

There is a time for many words, and there is also a time for sleep.

— Homer

Young Gorillas ride on their mothers' backs when they are about four months old, and some continue to do this until they are two years old. Every night lowland gorillas make nests to sleep in. They weave branches and leaves together into a circular bowl. A mother gorilla and her baby may share a nest for up to five years.